Benjamin Franklin: Quotes & Facts

By Blago Kirov

First Edition

Translated by Raia Iotova

*****

Benjamin Franklin: Quotes & Facts
*****

D1738629

Foreword

"If you're going through hell, keep going."

This book is an anthology of quotes from Benjamin Franklin and selected facts about Benjamin Franklin.

"There never was a good knife made of bad steel."

"Either write something worth reading or do something worth writing."

"Three may keep a secret, if two of them are dead."

"A Penny Saved is a Penny Earned"

"I didn't fail the test, I just found 100 ways to do it wrong."

"Many people die at twenty five and aren't buried until they are seventy five."

"If everyone is thinking alike, then no one is thinking."

"The heart of a fool is in his mouth, but the mouth of a wise man is in his heart."

"Any fool can criticize, condemn and complain and most fools do."

"Work as if you were to live a thousand years, play as if you were to die tomorrow."

Benjamin Franklin was born on Milk Street, in Boston, Massachusetts, on January 17, 1706.

Benjamin Franklin was one of seventeen children born to Josiah Franklin, and one of ten born by Josiah's second wife, Abiah Folger.

Although his parents talked of the church as a career for Franklin, his schooling ended when he was ten.

Franklin was an advocate of free speech from an early age.

Even after Franklin had achieved fame as a scientist and statesman, he habitually signed his letters with the unpretentious 'B. Franklin, Printer.'

Franklin invented the first newspaper chain.

In 1734, indicating Franklin edited and published the first Masonic book in the Americas.

In 1730, at the age of 24, Franklin publicly acknowledged the existence of William, his son, who was deemed 'illegitimate'.

Franklin frequently wrote under pseudonyms.

Among Franklin's many creations were the lightning rod, glass armonica (a glass instrument, not to be confused with the metal harmonica), Franklin stove, bifocal glasses and the flexible urinary catheter.

Franklin never patented his inventions.

Franklin was an avid chess player.

Franklin is the only Founding Father who is a signatory of all four of the major documents of the founding of the United States: the Declaration of Independence, the Treaty of Alliance with France, the Treaty of Paris and the United States Constitution.

Some Facts about Benjamin Franklin

Benjamin Franklin was one of the Founding Fathers of
the United States.

Benjamin Franklin was a renowned polymath, a leading author, printer, political theorist, politician, freemason, postmaster, scientist, inventor, civic activist, statesman, and diplomat.

As a scientist, Benjamin Franklin was a major figure in the American Enlightenment and the history of physics for his discoveries and theories regarding electricity.

As an inventor, Benjamin Franklin is known for the lightning rod, bifocals, and the Franklin stove, among other inventions.

Benjamin Franklin facilitated many civic organizations, including Philadelphia's fire department and a university.

Benjamin Franklin was born on Milk Street, in Boston, Massachusetts, on January 17, 1706, and baptized at Old South Meeting House.

Benjamin Franklin was one of seventeen children born to Josiah Franklin, and one of ten born by Josiah's second wife, Abiah Folger; the daughter of Peter Foulger and Mary Morrill.

His father wanted Benjamin to attend school with the clergy, but only had enough money to send him to school for two years.

Benjamin Franklin attended Boston Latin School but did not graduate; he continued his education through voracious reading.

Although his parents talked of the church as a career for Franklin, his schooling ended when he was ten.

Benjamin Franklin worked for his father for a time, and at 12 he became an apprentice to his brother James, a printer, who taught Ben the printing trade.

When Benjamin was 15, his brother James founded The New-England Courant, which was the first truly independent newspaper in the colonies.

When denied the chance to write a letter to the paper for publication, Franklin adopted the pseudonym of "Mrs. Silence Dogood", a middle-aged widow. Mrs. Dogood's letters were published, and became a subject of conversation around town. Neither James nor the Courant's readers were aware of the ruse, and James was unhappy with Ben when he discovered the popular correspondent was his younger brother.

Franklin was an advocate of free speech from an early age. When his brother was jailed for three weeks in 1722 for publishing material unflattering to the governor, young Franklin took over the newspaper and had Mrs. Dogood proclaim: "Without freedom of thought there can be no such thing as wisdom and no such thing as public liberty without freedom of speech."

Franklin left his apprenticeship without his brother's permission, and in so doing became a fugitive.

At age 17, Franklin ran away to Philadelphia, Pennsylvania, seeking a new start in a new city. When he first arrived, he worked in several printer shops around town, but he was not satisfied by the immediate prospects.

While working in a printing house, Franklin was convinced by Pennsylvania Governor Sir William Keith to go to London, ostensibly to acquire the equipment necessary for establishing another newspaper in Philadelphia. Finding Keith's promises of backing a newspaper empty, Franklin worked as a typesetter in a printer's shop in what is now the Church of St Bartholomew-the-Great in the Smithfield area of London.

He returned from London to Philadelphia in 1726 with the help of Thomas Denham, a merchant who employed Franklin as clerk, shopkeeper, and bookkeeper in his business.

In 1727, Benjamin Franklin, then 21, created the Junto, a group of "like minded aspiring artisans and tradesmen who hoped to improve themselves while they improved their community." The Junto was a discussion group for issues of the day; it subsequently gave rise to many organizations in Philadelphia. The Junto was modeled after English coffeehouses that Franklin knew well, and which should become the center of the spread of Enlightenment ideas in Britain.

Franklin conceived the idea of a subscription library, which would pool the funds of the members to buy books for all to read. This was the birth of the Library Company of Philadelphia: its charter was composed by Franklin in 1731. In 1732, Franklin hired the first American librarian, Louis Timothee. The Library Company is now a great scholarly and research library.

In 1728, Franklin had set up a printing house in partnership with Hugh Meredith; the following year he became the publisher of a newspaper called The Pennsylvania Gazette.

Even after Franklin had achieved fame as a scientist and statesman, he habitually signed his letters with the unpretentious 'B. Franklin, Printer.'

In 1732, Ben Franklin published the first German language newspaper in America – Die Philadelphische Zeitung – although it failed after only one year, because four other newly founded German papers quickly dominated the newspaper market.

Franklin printed Moravian religious books in German.

Franklin invented the first newspaper chain. It was more than a business venture, for like many publishers since, he believed that the press had a public-service duty.

Franklin was busy with a hundred matters outside of his printing office, and never seriously attempted to raise the mechanical standards of his trade.

In 1731, Franklin was initiated into the local Masonic Lodge. He became Grand Master in 1734.

In 1734, indicating Franklin edited and published the first Masonic book in the Americas, a reprint of James Anderson's Constitutions of the Free-Masons.

Franklin remained a Freemason for the end of his life.

In 1723, at the age of 17, Franklin proposed to 15-year-old Deborah Read while a boarder in the Read home. At that time, Read's mother was wary of allowing her young daughter to marry Franklin, who was on his way to London at Governor Sir William Keith's request, and also because of his financial instability. Her own husband had recently died, and Mrs. Read declined Franklin's request to marry her daughter.

Franklin established a common-law marriage with Deborah Read on September 1, 1730. They took in Franklin's young, recently acknowledged illegitimate son, William, and raised him in their household. In addition, they had two children together. The first, Francis Folger Franklin, born October 1732, died of smallpox in 1736. Their second child, Sarah Franklin, familiarly called Sally, was born in 1743.

Deborah Read Franklin died of a stroke in 1774, while Franklin was on an extended mission to England; he returned in 1775.

In 1730, at the age of 24, Franklin publicly acknowledged the existence of William, his son, who was deemed 'illegitimate' as he was born out of wedlock, and raised him in his household. His mother's identity is not known.

In 1733, Franklin began to publish the noted Poor Richard's Almanack (with content both original and borrowed) under the pseudonym Richard Saunders, on which much of his popular reputation is based.

Franklin frequently wrote under pseudonyms.

In 1741 Franklin began publishing The General Magazine and Historical Chronicle for all the British Plantations in America, the first such monthly magazine of this type published in America.

Franklin's autobiography, begun in 1771 but published after his death, has become one of the classics of the genre.

In 1758, Franklin printed Father Abraham's Sermon, also known as The Way to Wealth.

Among Franklin's many creations were the lightning rod, glass armonica (a glass instrument, not to be confused with the metal harmonica), Franklin stove, bifocal glasses and the flexible urinary catheter.

Franklin never patented his inventions.

In the 1730s and 1740s, Franklin began taking notes on population growth, finding that the American population had the fastest growth rates on earth. He calculated that America's population was doubling every twenty years and would surpass that of England in a century.

In 1751, Franklin drafted "Observations concerning the Increase of Mankind, Peopling of Countries, &c." Four years later, it was anonymously printed in Boston, and it was quickly reproduced in Britain, where it influenced the economists Adam Smith and later Thomas Malthus.

Franklin proposed that "vitreous" and "resinous" electricity were not different types of "electrical fluid" (as electricity was called then), but the same electrical fluid under different pressures. He was the first to label them as positive and negative respectively, and he was the first to discover the principle of conservation of charge

In 1750, Franklin published a proposal for an experiment to prove that lightning is electricity by flying a kite in a storm that appeared capable of becoming a lightning storm. On May 10, 1752, Thomas-François Dalibard of France conducted Franklin's experiment using a 40-foot-tall (12 m) iron rod instead of a kite, and he extracted electrical sparks from a cloud. On June 15 Franklin may possibly have conducted his well known kite experiment in Philadelphia, successfully extracting sparks from a cloud. Franklin's experiment was not written up with credit until Joseph Priestley's 1767 History and Present Status of Electricity; the evidence shows that Franklin was insulated (not in a conducting path, where he would have been in danger of electrocution).

Franklin's electrical experiments led to his invention of the lightning rod.

Following a series of experiments on Franklin's own house, lightning rods were installed on the Academy of Philadelphia (later the University of Pennsylvania) and the Pennsylvania State House (later Independence Hall) in 1752.

In recognition of his work with electricity, Franklin received the Royal Society's Copley Medal in 1753, and in 1756 he became one of the few 18th-century Americans elected as a Fellow of the Society.

The cgs unit of electric charge has been named after Franklin: one franklin (Fr) is equal to one statcoulomb.

Franklin was, along with his contemporary Leonhard Euler, the only major scientist who supported Christiaan Huygens' wave theory of light, which was basically ignored by the rest of the scientific community. In the 18th century Newton's corpuscular theory was held to be true; only after Young's well known slit experiment in 1803 was most scientists persuaded to believe Huygens' theory.

After the Icelandic volcanic eruption of Laki in 1783, and the subsequent harsh European winter of 1784, Franklin made observations connecting the causal nature of these two separate events. He wrote about them in a lecture series.

Franklin noted a principle of refrigeration by observing that on a very hot day, he stayed cooler in a wet shirt in a breeze than he did in a dry one. To understand this phenomenon more clearly Franklin conducted experiments.

Franklin is known to have played the violin, the harp, and the guitar. He also composed music, notably a string quartet in early classical style.

Franklin was an avid chess player. He was playing chess by around 1733, making him the first chess player known by name in the American colonies.

Franklin and a friend used chess as a means of learning the Italian language, which both were studying; the winner of each game between them had the right to assign a task, such as parts of the Italian grammar to be learned by heart, to be performed by the loser before their next meeting.

Franklin was able to play chess more frequently against stronger opposition during his many years as a civil servant and diplomat in England, where the game was far better established than in America. He was able to improve his playing standard by facing more experienced players during this period. He regularly attended the Old Slaughter's Coffee House in London for chess and socializing, making many important personal contacts.

While in Paris, both as a visitor and later as ambassador, Franklin visited the famous Café de la Régence, which France's strongest players made their regular meeting place. No records of his games have survived, so it is not possible to ascertain his playing strength in modern terms.

Franklin was inducted into the U.S. Chess Hall of Fame in 1999.

In 1736, Franklin created the Union Fire Company, one of the first volunteer firefighting companies in America.

Throughout his career, Franklin was an advocate for paper money, publishing A Modest Enquiry into the Nature and Necessity of a Paper Currency in 1729, and his printer printed money.

In 1743, Franklin founded the American Philosophical Society to help scientific men discuss their discoveries and theories.

In October 1748, Franklin was selected as a councilman, in June 1749 he became a Justice of the Peace for Philadelphia, and in 1751 he was elected to the Pennsylvania Assembly.

On August 10, 1753, Franklin was appointed deputy postmaster-general of British North America. His most notable service in domestic politics was his reform of the postal system, with mail sent out every week.

In 1751, Franklin and Dr. Thomas Bond obtained a charter from the Pennsylvania legislature to establish a hospital. Pennsylvania Hospital was the first hospital in what was to become the United States of America.

In 1756, Franklin organized the Pennsylvania Militia. He used Tun Tavern as a gathering place to recruit a regiment of soldiers to go into battle against the Native American uprisings that beset the American colonies. Reportedly Franklin was elected "Colonel" of the Associated Regiment but declined the honor.

Franklin was elected Speaker of the Pennsylvania House in May 1764.

In London, Franklin opposed the 1765 Stamp Act.

In 1756, Franklin had become a member of the Society for the Encouragement of Arts, Manufactures & Commerce (now the Royal Society of Arts or RSA), which had been founded in 1754 and whose early meetings took place in Covent Garden coffee shops.

In 1762, Oxford University awarded Franklin an honorary doctorate for his scientific accomplishments; from then on he went by "Doctor Franklin".

While living in London in 1768, he developed a phonetic alphabet in A Scheme for a new Alphabet and a Reformed Mode of Spelling. This reformed alphabet discarded six letters Franklin regarded as redundant (c, j, q, w, x, and y), and substituted six new letters for sounds he felt lacked letters of their own. His new alphabet, however, never caught on, and he eventually lost interest

In Dublin, Franklin was invited to sit with the members of the Irish Parliament rather than in the gallery. He was the first American to receive this honor.

Franklin spent two months in German lands in 1766, but his connections to the country stretched across a lifetime. He declared a debt of gratitude to German scientist Otto von Guericke for his early studies of electricity.

Franklin co-authored the first treaty of friendship between Prussia and America in 1785.

In September 1767, Franklin visited Paris with his usual traveling partner, Sir John Pringle. News of his electrical discoveries was widespread in France. His reputation meant that he was introduced to many influential scientists and politicians, and also to King Louis XV.

By the time Franklin arrived in Philadelphia on May 5, 1775, after his second mission to Great Britain, the American Revolution had begun – with fighting between colonials and British at Lexington and Concord. The New England militia had trapped the main British army in Boston. The Pennsylvania Assembly unanimously chose Franklin as their delegate to the Second Continental Congress. In June 1776, he was appointed a member of the Committee of Five that drafted the Declaration of Independence.

In December 1776, Franklin was dispatched to France as commissioner for the United States. He took with him as secretary his 16-year-old grandson, William Temple Franklin. They lived in a home in the Parisian suburb of Passy, donated by Jacques-Donatien Le Ray de Chaumont, who supported the United States. Franklin remained in France until 1785. He conducted the affairs of his country toward the French nation with great success, which included securing a critical military alliance in 1778 and negotiating the Treaty of Paris (1783).

Franklin also served as American minister to Sweden, although he never visited that country. He negotiated a treaty that was signed in April 1783.

On August 27, 1783, in Paris, Franklin witnessed the world's first hydrogen balloon flight. Le Globe, created by professor Jacques Charles and Les Frères Robert, was watched by a vast crowd as it rose from the Champ de Mars (now the site of the Eiffel Tower). This so enthused Franklin that he subscribed financially to the next project to build a manned hydrogen balloon.

When he returned home in 1785, Franklin occupied a position only second to that of George Washington as the champion of American independence.

After his return, Franklin became an abolitionist and freed his two slaves. He became president of the Pennsylvania Abolition Society.

In 1787, Franklin served as a delegate to the Philadelphia Convention. He held an honorary position and seldom engaged in debate.

Franklin is the only Founding Father who is a signatory of all four of the major documents of the founding of the United States: the Declaration of Independence, the Treaty of Alliance with France, the Treaty of Paris and the United States Constitution.

In 1787, a group of prominent ministers in Lancaster, Pennsylvania, proposed the foundation of a new college named in Franklin's honor. Franklin donated £200 towards the development of Franklin College (now called Franklin & Marshall College).

In 1790, Quakers from New York and Pennsylvania presented their petition for abolition to Congress. Their argument against slavery was backed by the Pennsylvania Abolitionist Society and its president, Benjamin Franklin.

Special balloting conducted October 18, 1785, unanimously elected Franklin the sixth president of the Supreme Executive Council of Pennsylvania, replacing John Dickinson. The office was practically that of governor. Franklin held that office for slightly over three years, longer than any other, and served the constitutional limit of three full terms.

When Franklin met Voltaire in Paris and asked this great apostle of the Enlightenment to bless his grandson, Voltaire said in English, "God and Liberty," and added, "this is the only appropriate benediction for the grandson of Monsieur Franklin."

Franklin clarified himself as a deist in his 1771 autobiography, although he still considered himself a Christian.

On July 4, 1776, Congress appointed a three-member committee composed of Franklin, Thomas Jefferson, and John Adams to design the Great Seal of the United States. Franklin's proposal (which was not adopted) featured the motto: "Rebellion to Tyrants is Obedience to God" and a scene from the Book of Exodus, with Moses, the Israelites, the pillar of fire, and George III depicted as pharaoh. The design that was produced was never acted upon by Congress, and the Great Seal's design was not finalized until a third committee was appointed in 1782.

Franklin sought to cultivate his character by a plan of 13 virtues, which he developed at age 20 (in 1726) and continued to practice in some form for the rest of his life.

Franklin struggled with obesity throughout his middle-aged and later years, which resulted in multiple health problems, particularly gout, which worsened as he aged.

Benjamin Franklin died from pleuritic attack at his home in Philadelphia on April 17, 1790, at age 84. Approximately 20,000 people attended his funeral.

Franklin was interred in Christ Church Burial Ground in Philadelphia.

In 1728, aged 22, Franklin wrote what he hoped would be his own epitaph:

The Body of B. Franklin Printer; Like the Cover of an old Book, Its Contents torn out, And stript of its Lettering and Gilding, Lies here, Food for Worms. But the Work shall not be wholly lost: For it will, as he believ'd, appear once more, In a new & more perfect Edition, Corrected and Amended By the Author.

His Words

"If you're going through hell, keep going."

"There never was a good knife made of bad steel."

"Either write something worth reading or do something worth writing."

"Three may keep a secret, if two of them are dead."

"A Penny Saved is a Penny Earned"

"I didn't fail the test, I just found 100 ways to do it wrong."

"Many people die at twenty five and aren't buried until they are seventy five."

"If everyone is thinking alike, then no one is thinking."

"The heart of a fool is in his mouth, but the mouth of a wise man is in his heart."

"Any fool can criticize, condemn and complain and most fools do."

"Work as if you were to live a thousand years, play as if you were to die tomorrow."

"They who can give up essential liberty to obtain a little temporary safety deserve neither liberty nor safety."

"Tell me and I forget, teach me and I may remember, involve me and I learn."

"He that can have patience can have what he will."

"Fear not death for the sooner we die, the longer we shall be immortal."

"In wine there is wisdom, in beer there is Freedom, in water there is bacteria."

"You may delay, but time will not."

"Never ruin an apology with an excuse."

"We are all born ignorant, but one must work hard to remain stupid."

"Beer is proof that God loves us and wants us to be happy."

"How many observe Christ's birthday! How few, His precepts!"

"Justice will not be served until those who are unaffected are as outraged as those who are."

"Well done is better than well said."

"By failing to prepare, you are preparing to fail."

"Those who surrender freedom for security will not have, nor do they deserve, either one."

"The Constitution only guarantees the American people the right to pursue happiness. You have to catch it yourself."

"Instead of cursing the darkness, light a candle."

"If all printers were determined not to print anything till they were sure it would offend nobody, there would be very little printed."

"An investment in knowledge pays the best interest."

"It is the first responsibility of every citizen to question authority."

"I am for doing good to the poor, but...I think the best way of doing good to the poor, is not making them easy in poverty, but leading or driving them out of it. I observed...that the more public provisions were made for the poor, the less they provided for themselves, and of course became poorer. And, on the contrary, the less was done for them, the more they did for themselves, and became richer."

"Being ignorant is not so much a shame, as being unwilling to learn."

"Be at war with your vices, at peace with your neighbors, and let every new year find you a better man."

"The person who deserves most pity is a lonesome one on a rainy day who doesn't know how to read."

"Dost thou love life? Then do not squander time, for that's the stuff life is made of."

"Remember not only to say the right thing in the right place, but far more difficult still, to leave unsaid the wrong thing at the tempting moment."

"There was never a bad peace or a good war."

"Man will occasionally stumble over the truth, but usually manages to pick himself up, walk over or around it, and carry on."

"Never confuse Motion with Action."

"Early to bed and early to rise makes a man healthy, wealthy, and wise."

"Educate your children to self-control, to the habit of holding passion and prejudice and evil tendencies subject to an upright and reasoning will, and you have done much to abolish misery from their future and crimes from society."

"Be slow in choosing a friend, slower in changing."

"Whatever is begun in anger, ends in shame."

"A slip of the foot you may soon recover, but a slip of the tongue you may never get over."

"When you are finished changing, you're finished."

"Trouble knocked at the door, but, hearing laughter, hurried away"

"Lost time is never found again"

"When you're testing to see how deep water is, never use two feet."

"Certainty? In this world nothing is certain but death and taxes."

"He that is good for making excuses is seldom good for anything else."

"Do not anticipate trouble, or worry about what may never happen. Keep in the sunlight."

"If Jack's in love, he's no judge of Jill's beauty."

"Energy and persistence conquers all things"

"To find out a girl's faults, praise her to her girlfriends."

"Lighthouses are more helpful than churches."

"I agree to this Constitution with all its faults, if they are such: because I think a General Government necessary for us, and there is no Form of Government but what may be a Blessing to the People if well-administred; and I believe farther that this is likely to be well administred for a Course of Years and can only end in Despotism as other Forms have done before it, when the People shall become so corrupted as to need Despotic Government, being incapable of any other."

"Life biggest tragedy is that we get old too soon and wise too late"

"Happiness depends more on the inward disposition of mind than on outward circumstances."

"Keep your eyes wide open before marriage, half shut afterwards."

"We must all hang together, or assuredly we shall all hang separately."

"If a man could have half of his wishes, he would double his troubles."

"Be civil to all; sociable to many; familiar with few; friend to one; enemy to none."

"While we may not be able to control all that happens to us, we can control what happens inside us."

"Who is wise? He that learns from everyone. Who is powerful? He that governs his passions. Who is rich? He that is content. Who is that? Nobody."

"A house is not a home unless it contains food and fire for the mind as well as the body."

"Flesh eating is unprovoked murder."

"Contentment makes poor men rich, Discontent makes rich men poor."

"Speak ill of no man, but speak all the good you know of everybody."

"The best thing to give to your enemy is forgiveness; to an opponent, tolerance; to a friend, your heart; to your child, a good example; to a father, deference; to your mother, conduct that will make her proud of you; to yourself, respect; to all others, charity."

"When the people find that they can vote themselves money that will herald the end of the republic."

"Never leave till tomorrow that which you can do today."

"All mankind is divided into three classes: those that are immovable, those that are movable, and those that move."

"When the well is dry, we know the worth of water."

"Whoever would overthrow the liberty of a nation must begin by subduing the freeness of speech."

"To be humble to superiors is a duty, to equals courtesy, to inferiors nobleness."

"The way to see by faith is to shut the eye of reason."

"Security without liberty is called prison."

"A Brother may not be a Friend, but a Friend will always be a Brother."

"Love your Enemies, for they tell you your Faults."

"Fish and visitors smell in three days."

"I have lived, Sir, a long time and the longer I live, the more convincing proofs I see of this truth -- that God governs in the affairs of men. And if a sparrow cannot fall to the ground without his notice, is it probable that an empire can rise without his aid? We have been assured, Sir, in the sacred writings that "except the Lord build they labor in vain that build it." I firmly believe this; and I also believe that without his concurring aid we shall succeed in this political building no better than the Builders of Babel"

"The problem with doing nothing is not knowing when your finished."

"Believe none of what you hear, and only half of what you see."

"We do not stop playing because we grow old, we grow old because we stop playing!"

"Those things that hurt, instruct."

"It takes many good deeds to build a good reputation, and only one bad one to lose it."

"If you would not be forgotten, as soon as you are dead and rotten, either write things worth reading, or do things worth the writing."

"Words may show a man's wit, actions his meaning."

"All the little money that ever came into my hands was ever laid out in books."

"A good example is the best sermon."

"An ounce of prevention is worth a pound of cure."

"Genius without education is like silver in the mine."

"Eat to live, don't live to eat."

"The only thing that is more expensive than education is ignorance."

"No one cares what you know until they know that you care!"

"Fools make feasts and wise men eat them."

"Many a man thinks he is buying pleasure, when he is really selling himself to it."

"There are three things extremely hard: steel, a diamond, and to know one's self."

"For the best return on your money, pour your purse into your head."

"Beware of little expenses; a small leak will sink a great ship."

"How few there are who have courage enough to own their faults, or resolution enough to mend them."

"Women are books, and men the readers be..."

"Reading makes a full man, meditation a profound man, discourse a clear man."

"Happiness consists more in the small conveniences of pleasures that occur every day, than in great pieces of good fortune that happen but seldom to a man in the course of his life."

"Absence sharpens love, presence strengthens it."

"To cease to think creatively is to cease to live"

"He who can have patience can have what he will."

"You will find the key to success under the alarm clock."

"Anger is never without a reason, but seldom with a good one"

"To lengthen thy life, lessen thy meals."

"Fear God, and your enemies will fear you."

"One today is worth two tomorrows"

"A false friend and a shadow attend only while the sun shines."

"You only have the right to pursue happiness; you have to catch it yourself."

"A Man convinced against his will is of the same opinion still."

"The way to wealth is as plain as the way to market. It depends chiefly on two words, industry and frugality: that is, waste neither time nor money, but make the best use of both. Without industry and frugality nothing will do, and with them everything."

"The best way to see Faith is to shut the eye of Reason."

"It is with great sincerity I join you in acknowledging and admiring the dispensations of Providence in our favor. America has only to be thankful and to persevere. God will finish his work and establish their freedom.... If it had not been for the justice of our cause, and the consequent interposition of Providence, in which we had faith, we must have been ruined. If had ever before been an atheist, I should now have been convinced of the being and government of a Deity! It is He who abases the proud and favors the humble. May we never forget His goodnes to us, and may our future conduct manifest our gratitude....I believe in one God, Creator of the universe. That He governs it by his providence. That He ought to be worshiped."

"He that speaks much, is much mistaken."

"He that won't be counseled can't be helped."

"Most people die at 25 and aren't buried until they're 75."

"If you fail to plan, you are planning to fail!"

"There cannot be good living where there is not good drinking."

"For every minute spent in organizing, an hour is earned."

"Fart for freedom, fart for liberty — and fart proudly."

"Sloth makes all things difficult, but industry all easy; and he that riseth late must trot all day, and shall scarce overtake his business at night; while laziness travels so slowly, that poverty soon overtakes him."

"You can do anything you set your mind to"

"Critics are our friends, they show us our faults."

"He that falls in love with himself will have no rivals."

"A learned blockhead is a greater blockhead than an ignorant one."

"If Passion drives, let Reason hold the Reins."

"There will be plenty of time to sleep once you are dead"

"An apple a day keeps the doctor away."

"Don't cry over spilled milk"

"If you would be loved, love, and be loveable."

"Glass, China, and Reputation, are easily cracked, and never well mended."

"Blessed is he who expects nothing, for he shall never be disappointed."

"Tricks and treachery are the practice of fools that don't have brains enough to be honest."

"All highly competent people continually search for ways to keep learning, growing, and improving. They do that by asking WHY. After all, the person who knows HOW will always have a job, but the person who knows WHY will always be the boss."

"Joy is not in things, it is in us."

"When the well is dry we know the value of water"

"Thinking aloud is a habit which is responsible for most of mankind's misery."

"The securest place is a prison cell, but there is no liberty"

"Be studious in your profession, and you will be learned. Be industrious and frugal, and you will be rich. Be sober and temperate, and you will be healthy. Be in general virtuous, and you will be happy. At least you will, by such conduct, stand the be."

"God grant that not only the love of liberty but a thorough knowledge of the rights of man may pervade all the nations of the earth, so that anybody may set his foot anywhere on its surface and say: 'This is my country!"

"Genius is nothing but a greater aptitude for patience."

"Haste makes waste."

"Without Freedom of thought there can be no such thing as wisdom;and no such thing as public liberty, without freedom of speech."

"Without continual growth and progress, such words as improvement, achievement, and success have no meaning."

"A man wrapped up in himself makes a very small bundle."

"He that lives upon hope will die fasting."

"A place for everything, everything in its place".

"Where there's marriage without love, there will be love without marriage."

"The people heard it, and approved the doctrine, and immediately practiced the contrary."

"He that displays too often his wife and his wallet is in danger of having both of them borrowed."

"A nation of well-informed men who have been taught to know and prize the rights which God has given them cannot be enslaved. It is in the region of ignorance that tyranny begins."

"All would live long, but none would be old."

"He that has once done you a kindness will be more ready to do you another, than he whom you yourself have obliged."

"He that blows the coals in quarrels that he has nothing to do with, has no right to complain if the sparks fly in his face."

"He that is the opinion money will do everything may well be suspected of doing everything for money."

"Old boys have their playthings as well as young ones; the difference is only in the price."

"Money has never made man happy, nor will it; There is nothing in its nature to produce happiness. The more of it one has, the more one wants."

"Who is rich? He that is content. Who is that? Nobody."

"God helps them that help themselves."

"Perhaps I'm too saucy or provoking?"

"He that would live in peace and at ease, must not speak all he knows nor judge all he sees."

"A man must have a good deal of vanity who believes, and a good deal of boldness who affirms, that all the doctrines he holds are true, and all he rejects are false."

"Only a virtuous people are capable of freedom."

"If you have a bald head don't walk out in the sun because you will get burned."

"Serving God is doing good to man, but praying is thought an easier service and therefore more generally chosen."

"To be proud of virtue, is to poison yourself with the Antidote."

"A countryman between two lawyers is like a fish between two cats."

"The purpose of money was to purchase one's freedom to pursue that which is useful and interesting."

"Nothing ventured, nothing gained!!!"

"O powerful goodness! Bountiful Father! Merciful Guide! Increase in me that wisdom which discovers my truest interest. Strengthen my resolution to perform what that wisdom dictates. Accept my kind offices to thy other children as the only return in my power for thy continual favours to me. "

"If you know how to spend less than you get, you have the philosopher's stone."

"In reality, there is, perhaps, no one of our natural passions so hard to subdue as pride. Disguise it, struggle with it, beat it down, stifle it, mortify it as much as one pleases, it is still alive, and will every now and then peep out and show itself; you will see it, perhaps, often in this history; for, even if I could conceive that I had compleatly overcome it, I should probably be proud of my humility."

"Savages we call them, because their manners differ from ours, which we think the perfection of civility; they think the same of theirs. "

"God heals, and the doctor takes the fees."

"Nine men in ten are suicides."

"There are two ways to increase your wealth. Increase your means or decrease your wants. The best is to do both at the same time."

"Even peace may be purchased at too high a price."

"Write your injuries in dust, your benefits in marble."

"To all apparent beauties blind, each blemish strikes an envious mind."

"Vicious actions are not hurtful because they are forbidden, but forbidden because they are hurtful."

"After three days men grow weary, of a wench, a guest, and weather rainy."

"That which hurts, also instructs."

"The doorstep to the temple of wisdom is a knowledge of our own ignorance."

"Do not fear mistakes."

"To succeed, jump as quickly at opportunities as you do at conclusions."

"Do good to your friends to keep them, to your enemies to win them."

"I believe in one God, Creator of the Universe in that He ought to be whipped from pilar to post and back again for His shameful actions toward Humanity."

"If you will not be forgotten as soon as you are dead, then write something worth reading, or do something worth writing."

"Motivation is when your dreams put on work clothes"

"I wake up every morning at nine and grab for the morning paper. Then I look at the obituary page. If my name is not on it, I get up."

"Great beauty, great strength, and great riches are really and truly of no great use; a right heart exceeds all"

"If you would not be forgotten as soon as you are dead, either write something worth reading or do something worth writing."

"Liberality is not giving much, but giving wisely."

"A friend in need is a friend indeed!"

"Any society that would give up a little liberty to gain a little security will deserve neither and lose both."

"The discontented man finds no easy chair. "

"Be not sick too late, nor well too soon"

"The U.S. Constitution doesn't guarantee happiness, only the pursuit of it. Your have to catch up with it yourself."

"It is easier to suppress the first desire than to satisfy all that follow it."

"Don't put off until tomorrow what you can do today."

"Reading was the only amusement I allowed myself"

"Wise men don't need advice. Fools won't take it."

"He who is good at making excuses is seldom good at anything else."

"Any society that will give up a little liberty for a little security will deserve neither and lose both."

"Read much, but not many books."

"On the whole, though I never arrived at the perfection I had been so ambitious of obtaining, but fell far short of it, yet as I was, by the endeavor, a better and a happier man than I otherwise should have been had I not attempted it"

"Originality is the art of concealing your sources."

"If you would not be forgotten, as soon as you're dead and rotten, either do things worth the writing, or write things worth the reading!"

"Half-wits talk much, but say little."

"You have on hand those things that you need if you have but the wit and wisdom to use them."

"Experience keeps a dear school but fools will learn in no other"

Made in the USA
San Bernardino, CA
06 June 2016